How Many?

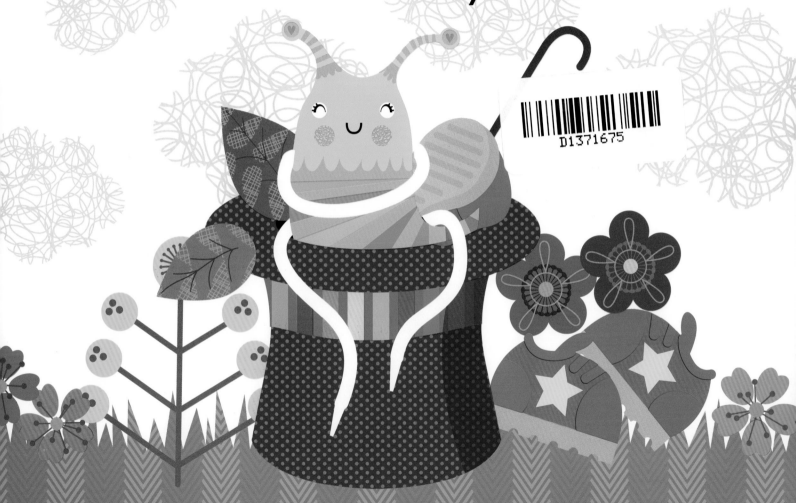

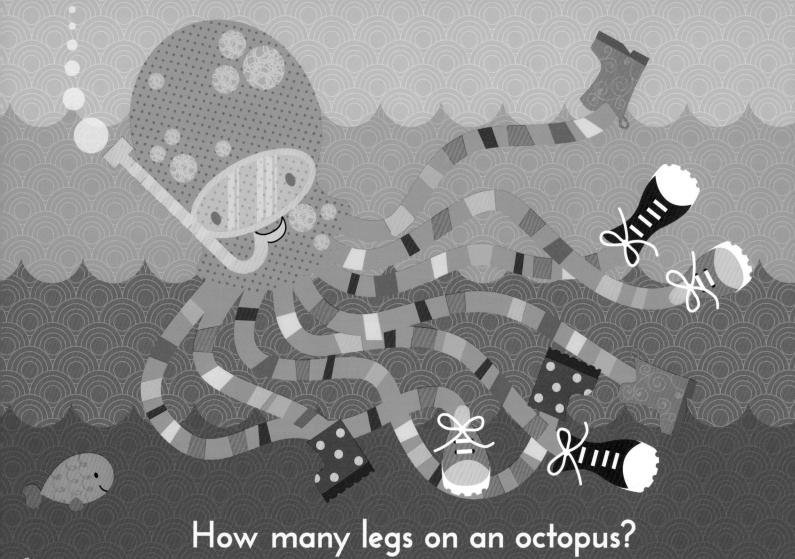

How many legs on an octopus?

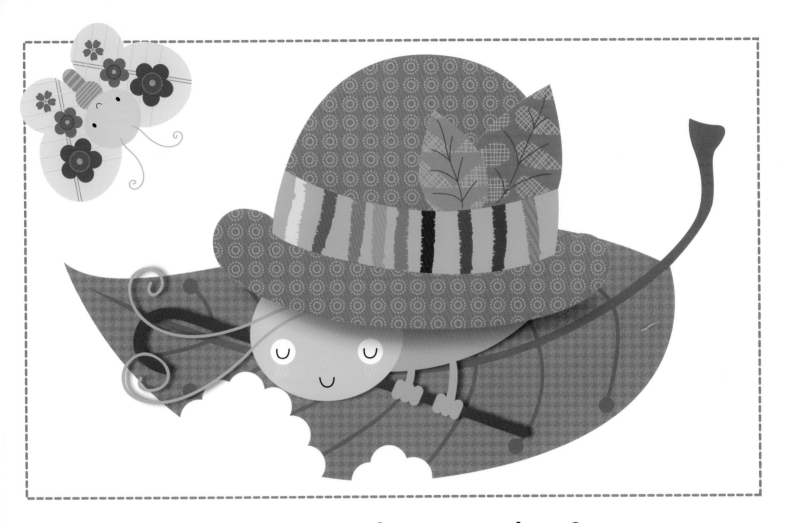

How many legs on a bug?

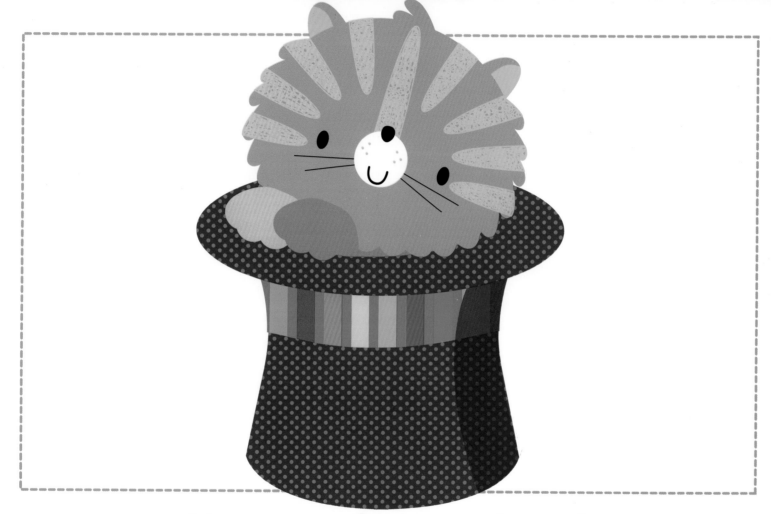

How many legs on a kitten?

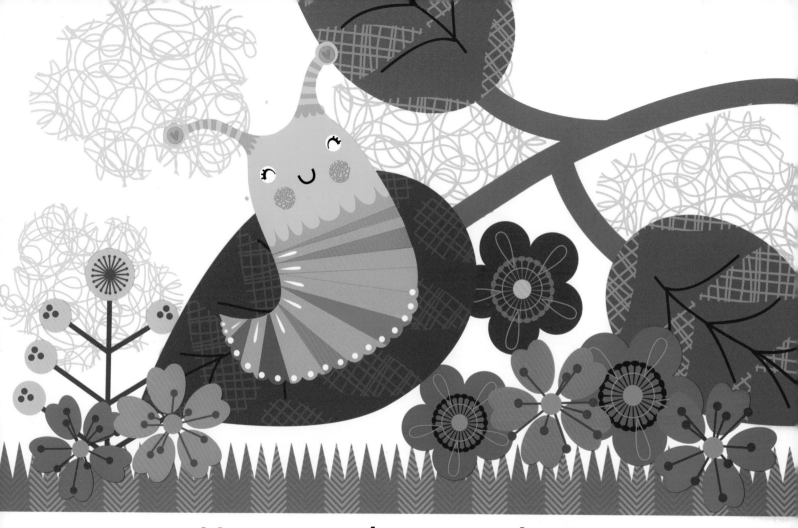

How many legs on a slug?

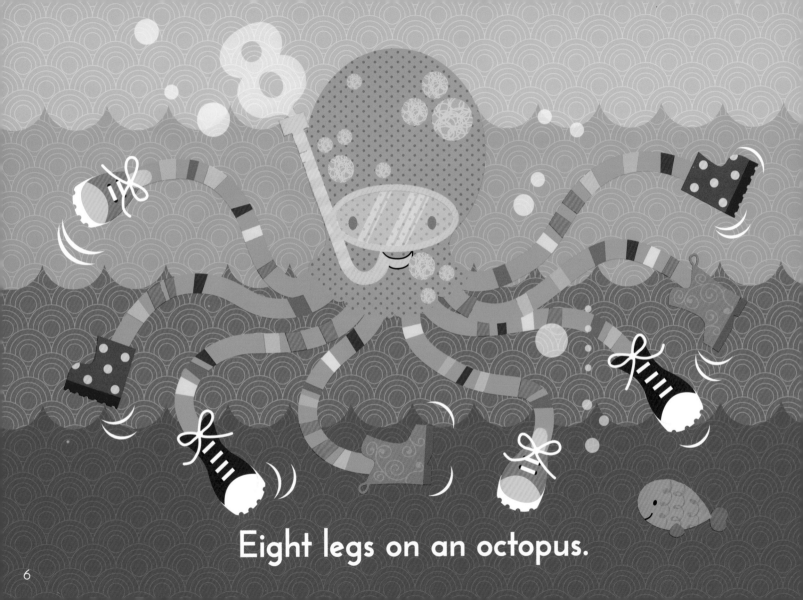

Eight legs on an octopus.

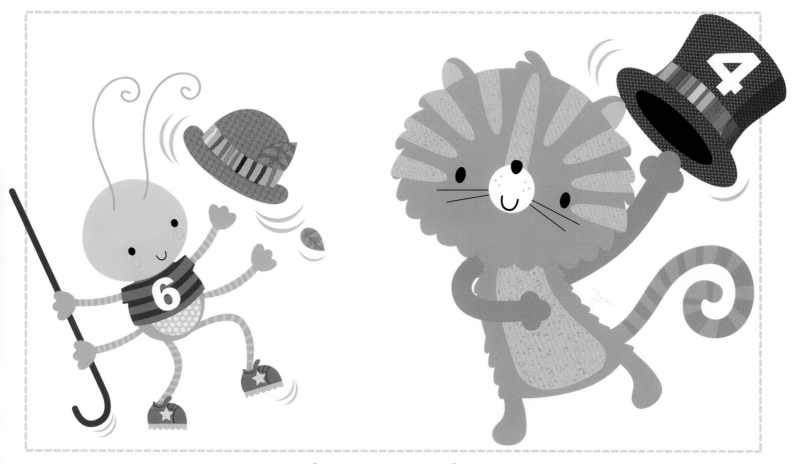

Six legs on a bug.
Four legs on a kitten.

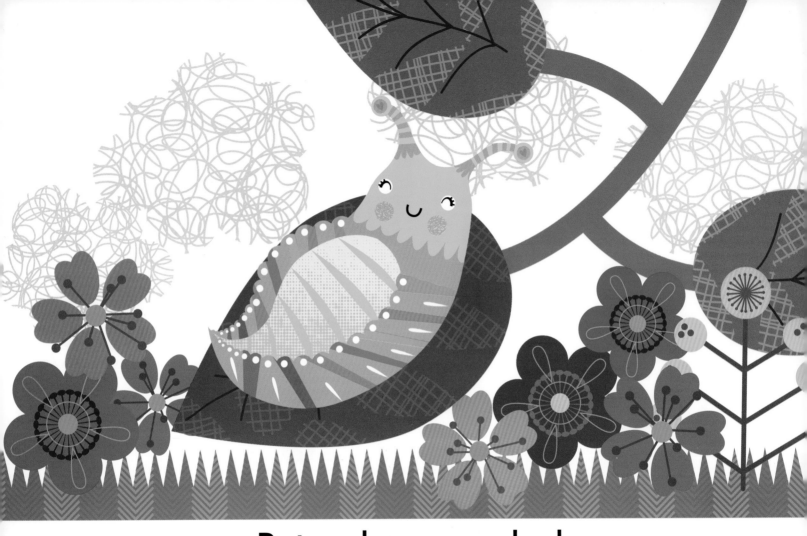

But no legs on a slug!